wishing you well

Also by June Cotner

wishing you well

PRAYERS AND POEMS

FOR COMFORT, HEALING,

AND RECOVERY

JUNE COTNER

LOYOLAPRESS.

CHICAGO

LOYOLAPRESS.

3441 N. ASHLAND AVENUE
CHICAGO, ILLINOIS 60657
(800) 621-1008
WWW.LOYOLABOOKS.ORG

Parts of this book were originally published in 2001 as *Get Well Wishes: Prayers, Poems, and Blessings* by HarperSanFrancisco, a division of HarperCollins Publishers Inc.

Reprint permissions begin on p. 147

Cover and interior design by Tracey Sainz

Library of Congress Cataloging-in-Publication Data

Wishing you well : prayers and poems for comfort, healing, and recovery / [compiled by] June Cotner.

    p.   cm.
  Includes index
  ISBN 0-8294-2036-3

  1. Sick—Prayer-books and devotions—English. 2. Healing—Prayer-books and devotions—English. 3. Prayers. 4. Sick—Poetry. 5. Healing—Poetry. 6. Consolation.   I. Cotner, June, 1950–
BV270.W57 2005
242'.4—dc22

                                             2004020781

Printed in the United States of America
05 06 07 08 09 10 Bang 10 9 8 7 6 5 4 3 2 1

Wishing You Well is dedicated
in memoriam to my dear friend,
who inspired all who knew him:

Brian Cox
(1950–1999)

This book is also dedicated to my friends who have fought
or still fight the daily battles that illness entails:

Virginia Lynn Eathorne
Joanie Guggenmos
Charlotte Carter Izett
Irma Kalman

I have great respect and admiration for your
grit, determination, and courage.
Thanks for helping me see that every day is truly a gift.
This book's for you . . . and please, be well.

contents

3 COURAGE

6 REFLECTIONS

7 GRATITUDE

8 INSPIRATION

Thanks

I'm very grateful to Joseph Durepos, senior acquisitions editor, and Jim Manney, trade editorial director, both at Loyola Press, for realizing the true potential of this book. I also appreciate the terrific support and help I have received from the staff at Loyola Press: Matthew S. Diener, managing editor; Melissa Crane, director of marketing; Leslie Waters, editorial assistant; and Erin Bechill, marketing coordinator. As always, I'm extremely thankful to my longtime agent and friend, Denise Marcil, for her untiring dedication to my books.

My husband Jim, my children Kyle and Kirsten, my sister Sue, and my closest friends continue to be constant sources of strength and support. You each enrich my life in so many ways, and I can't thank you enough.

None of my books would be possible without the poets who contribute their eloquent, insightful words to my collections. In addition to receiving several thousand submissions for each book, over 650 poets contribute to my books on a regular basis. I look forward to the arrival of your envelopes in my office. I always know when I sit down to read your submissions that I will be deeply moved and inspired. Your words truly help me to be a better person.

Beginning with my first anthology, *Graces,* I used a "test-market" group to help ensure that the selections were accessible to the general reader, inclusive enough to meet the satisfaction of three major religious beliefs, and poetic enough to please poets. To that end, I wish to thank the following individuals for participating in this process: Denise Marcil, Liz Perle, David Hennessy, and Joyce Standish. Representing three major religions, I also wish to thank Father Paul Keenan, Rabbi Rami M. Shapiro, and Reverend Gary W. Huffman. Representing the medical perspective, I wish to thank my physician, Patrick Tracy, MD; poet, anthologist, and psychiatrist, Janine Canan, MD; and my loving aunt, Ann Cotner, RN.

Deepest gratitude is owed to the following poets who lent their poetic talent to this project and gave me a careful critique: Barbara Crooker, Lori Eberhardy, Margaret Anne Huffman, Arlene Gay Levine, and Paula Timpson.

The highest recognition is due to the poets whose work appears in *Wishing You Well*. Your selections were chosen from thousands, and then had to meet the additional approval of my thirty-person "test-market" group. I'd also like to pay respect to the thousands of poets who submit for my projects, but who don't make the final cut. Your poems help enrich my life every day; I wish I could publish all of you! Please know that your words have sparked a reverberation in the universe. As poetry anthologist Kate Farrell states: "What poets and artists do lives after them and adds something to the world, becoming a sort of man-made natural resource, a permanent public repository of private visions of the many different ways human life has been and is and might be."

I wish to thank the following friends, relatives, and colleagues who participated in my "test-market" process: Virginia Lynn Eathorne, Brian Cox, Marjorie Cox, Cheryl Edmonson, Sue Gitch, Jim Graves, Joanie Guggenmos, Patricia Huckell, Charlotte Carter Izett, Irma Kalman, Barb Krell, Lacey Menne, Kirsten Casey, Sue Peterson, and John Standish. Your feedback was so helpful to me.

Also, I'm ever grateful to Suzanne Droppert, owner of Liberty Bay Books in Poulsbo, Washington, for all her support for my books, and to the staff of the Poulsbo Library for efficiently handling our many requests for books so we could track down original permission sources.

I wouldn't have the opportunity to continue to do this work I love without the readers who purchase my books. Thank you for your support that now has extended over a decade!

And most important, I'm grateful to God for work that brings continual joy to my life, and for helping me see that each day is a blessing.

A Letter to Readers

Twelve years ago, I had started a collection of poems and prayers (some of which are included in this book) that helped me cope with a difficult journey that began with a car accident that changed my life. In one moment, my athletic lifestyle was transformed into a sedentary one. A neck injury changed me into a fragile, disabled woman. Just opening a window caused tremendous pain.

My medication made me lethargic and severely impacted my thinking process and memory—and there were many other unpleasant side effects to cope with. One of the prescriptions that was supposed to "help my nerve endings heal" was actually an antidepressant. When I quit using it, cold turkey (not knowing it was an antidepressant), I sank into a depression, the state of a "lightless prison," which is so eloquently expressed by Arlene Gay Levine on p. 76.

Three years later, I still couldn't ride my bicycle because the weight of a bicycle helmet was overwhelming. Sometimes the road to wellness can be a long one—one that requires more than physical stamina to complete the journey.

I have arranged the chapters in *Wishing You Well* in an order that has personal significance for me. I found that when accident or illness strikes, we first need comfort—from whatever source; hopefully, from relatives and friends. But in those "3 AM" moments (see p. 19), when we feel most alone, often it is faith that helps pull us through our despair. Once we are strengthened by faith, we are fortified to move on toward rebuilding our lives.

But oh those initial steps are so difficult! It's then that giving up seems to be the easier path. May the selections in "Courage" offer a stepping-stone to start you on your road to discovering hope. For hope buoys our spirits, brings us optimism, and encourages us to go on so that the process of healing can begin.

As we improve, it's natural to reflect on the impact the accident or illness has had on our lives. It's a time of great contemplation. Shortly after my accident, it seemed that all I could do was bemoan "all I had lost." The words in my own prayer on

p. 139 gradually found their way into my soul—and as odd as it may seem, I began to experience glimmers of gratitude.

Gratitude sets the stage for inspiration. For me, the period of great physical inactivity led to a surprising burst of mental activity that eventually resulted in my writing career. I seriously doubt that the "pre-accident June" would have slowed down enough to take on the writing projects I enjoy today.

We never know what curves life will throw us. I hope the prayers, poems, and blessings in this book will bring you comfort, faith, courage, hope, healing, reflection, gratitude, and inspiration on your personal journey of recovery. Many have made the journey before you, but no one has experienced exactly what you are experiencing right now. May God's grace be with you. And may you be well.

June Cotner
P.O. Box 2765
Poulsbo, WA 98370
www.junecotner.com

1

comfort

Do Not Be Afraid

Do not be afraid—I will save you.
I have called you by name—you are mine.
When you pass through deep waters,
I will be with you; your troubles will not overwhelm you.

Isaiah 43:1–2
(Today's English Version)

Still Waters

May still waters surround you
in a harbor of peace.
Think dragonflies on summer afternoons,
cow and calf in farmer's field;
think summer sunsets,
autumn moons,
fog mist on morning ponds.
Think still waters
and find quiet rest
among the thoughts
of family and friends
who wish for you—
gentle love—
always.

Patricia M. Poland

Angel Promise

Wherever you are
　　I will be there,
Whatever might help
　　I can bring.
Dark hours alone
　　need not frighten,
Whatever will soothe
　　I shall sing.

Sara Sanderson

Unending Love

We are loved
by an unending love.
We are embraced
by arms that find us
even when
we are hidden from ourselves.
We are touched
by fingers that soothe us
even when
we are too proud for soothing.
We are counseled
by voices that guide us
even when
we are too embittered to hear.
We are loved
by an unending love.
We are supported
by hands that uplift us
even in
the midst of a fall.
We are urged on

by eyes that meet us
even when
we are too weak for meeting.
We are loved
by an unending love.

Rabbi Rami Shapiro

From Your Friend

For you I will pray—
every morning,
every morning and day,
every morning, day, and night;
and every time God
brings you to mind,
and every time in between that.
Just know, I will be praying—
without ceasing . . .

Jill Noblit MacGregor

To a Good Friend

Take my hand—it will not weaken me
Feel my warmth—it will not lessen
Touch my soul—it is there to be reached
Drink from my cup—there is always more
Absorb my caring—I feel part of your loss
Be strong in my strength—there's more than enough

Gwen Tremain Runyard

Angel Embrace

There are angels who sit quietly
and whisper when we need comfort.
There are those who breathe life into us
when we are breathless.

There are angels who fill us with gracious support
when our souls become fragile,
and those who kiss us goodnight for a peaceful slumber.

There are angels that touch us with sacred laughter
when tears become a burden.
There are those who wrap their wings around us
and rock us until the ache in our heart disappears.

There are angels that can send us flying with wonder
when our hope begins to fade,
and those who devote everything to give us
everlasting peace in heaven.

Lori Eberhardy

Each Day You Call My Heart, O God

Each day You call my heart, O God.
I hear You in the silver
afternoons of winter,
the winds that play like harps
in leafless trees. I hear You
in the snow that walks
like shoes of pearl in darkness
and in light. You keep me
company in every kind of loneliness.
In sickness
and in health You walk with me.
I hold Your stars inside my soul.
Each day You call my heart, O God,
For You are always near.

Marion Schoeberlein

A Quiet Comfort

I look up to the sky and I see
one star shining brightly.
I know it is you.

The breeze whispers in my ear,
"You are not alone. I am here with you."

I find comfort as your light shines on me
and covers me with a warm embrace.
As the rhythm of life eases my burdens,
I feel completely held by your grace.

Lori Eberhardy

Testing, Testing . . .

Such a simple phrase, "Let's run a few tests," and here I am, O God, shivering flimsy-gowned and alone, as scared of the tests as of their findings.

While I wait, cradle me as the wailing, lost child I've become. Closing my eyes and breathing deeply, I feel Your warming presence as a blanket tossed around my shoulders and know that no matter the bottom line being tallied up behind lead screens and computer consoles, You hold the most important truth, whispering it now, "You are my beloved child . . . I am with you."

Margaret Anne Huffman
(1941–2000)

The Lord Is My Shepherd

The Lord is my shepherd; I shall not want. He maketh me to lie down in green pastures: he leadeth me beside the still waters. He restoreth my soul: he leadeth me in the paths of righteousness for his name's sake. Yea, though I walk through the valley of the shadow of death, I will fear no evil: for thou art with me; thy rod and thy staff they comfort me. Thou preparest a table before me in the presence of mine enemies: thou anointest my head with oil; my cup runneth over. Surely goodness and mercy shall follow me all the days of my life: and I will dwell in the house of the Lord for ever.

Psalms 23:1–6
(King James Version)

The Light of God Surrounds Me

The light of God surrounds me;
The love of God enfolds me;
The power of God protects me;
The presence of God watches over me.
Wherever I am, God is.

Author unknown

Let Nothing Disturb You

Let nothing disturb you;
Let nothing dismay you.
All things pass;
God never changes.
Patience attains
All it strives for.
The one who has God
Finds that nothing is lacking.
God alone suffices.

Teresa of Ávila
(1515–1582)

Peace I Give unto You

Peace I leave with you,
my peace I give unto you:
not as the world giveth,
give I unto you.
Let not your heart be troubled,
neither let it be afraid.

John 14:27
(King James Version)

2

faith

A Life Jacket

Life has a way of surprising us.
It does not behave the way we
planned or anticipated.
That is when we grab on to faith
and hang on to it
like a life jacket
until better days.

Phyllis Joy Davison

3 AM

There is a place where we are alone.
It's called 3 AM.
3 AM is when the pain meds wear off.
3 AM is when sleep deserts you.
3 AM is when the silent movie of your life begins to roll in front of your staring eyes.
3 AM is when the deep, bone deep, gut deep, heart-wrenching grief of the things you haven't yet done explodes like a grenade. The foolishnesses you've committed. The words you can't take back. The things you didn't do because of fear. Hah! What was that fear compared to dying?

But I'll tell you a mystery.

Right there. Right then. Right in the middle of 3 AM.
Beside all the pain, physical and emotional.
Next to the dread
In the midst of deep wrenching grief:
God was with me.
Right there. Right beside me.
A presence.
Always.

Lo, God is with me.
And, I am not alone.

Sylvia LeFort Masi

Take My Hand

Hand in hand, dear God, we will make it through this lonely valley of illness, for I will not be alone. I will feel You in the hands of those who hold mine, who rub my back, wipe my feverish face, count out pills and potions to ease and heal; in the deft touch of those who bind up and patch my ailing body; in the consoling, uplifting, encircling hugs and embraces of family and friends.

Already I feel You near and am assured that wherever I am on this path of illness, Your strong hand is there to guide and to hold.

Margaret Anne Huffman
(1941–2000)

Steps

As disappointments slowly,
quietly stack like fallen leaves,
as sorrow finds you
cold and still like ice groaning
on the surface of the frozen lake,
listen for that voice
that has no sound, beloved.
After the wind calls your name
it will whisper in still moments
the words you long for.
The answer, the direction
the steps that lead you home.

Joan Shroyer-Keno

Hearing with Hearts of Faith

If the ocean can roar in the shell
I hold to my ear miles from any ocean,
I know that You,
God of time and tide,
can restore me,
stranded as I am
on this barren shore of illness.

Margaret Anne Huffman
(1941–2000)

Promise

God of life, there are days when the burdens we carry chafe our shoulders and wear us down; when the road seems dreary and endless, the skies gray and threatening; when our lives have no music in them and our hearts are lonely, and our souls have lost their courage. Flood the path with light, we beseech you; turn our eyes to where the skies are full of promise.

St. Augustine
(354–430)

Great Expectations

At times it is hard to see the light
through these shadows of doubt,
but there is hope in my soul.

With great expectations I reach past
the shadows that surround me.
I transcend the darkness and my spirit
becomes woven in the sunlight.

With tenderness I listen to the sweet
sounds of amazing grace,
and with the vision of a child,
I remind myself that
this is the day, the hour, the moment
to keep the faith.

Lori Eberhardy

Believe

When you come to the edge
Of all the light you know,

And are about to step off
Into the darkness of the unknown,

Faith is knowing
One of two things will happen:

There will be something solid to stand on,
Or you will be taught how to fly.

Author unknown

Prayer in Time of Trouble

God of Peace,
God of All Tranquillity,

Be for us Light
in all our darknesses.

Be for us Calm
in every storm.

Be for us Stillness
in our turmoil.

Let us rest in You,
as a child in
a mother's arms;
a nested bird.

And let Your Grace
now rest upon us,
as moonlight rests
upon the water;
as soft rain
falls to rest
on thirsty ground.

Let Your Grace
now rest
like gentle rain
upon us.

Deborah Gordon Cooper

Safe Passage

The touch of your hand comforts me.
The sound of your voice calms me.
My spirit is eager to fly free.
To break away from this fear that has become
a burden to me.
At times I feel like a prisoner and this
fear is painted thick on the walls that surround me.
So I find an open door and
on the other side is you.
I'm not surprised.
It's always you.
You tell me to take your hand.
You rescue me.

Lori Eberhardy

I Will Not Be Overcome

I know that at times I will be troubled,
I know that at times I will be belabored,
I know that at times I will be disquieted,
but I believe that I will not be overcome. Amen.

Julian of Norwich
(1342–ca. 1419)

Do Not Lose Heart

Therefore we do not lose heart.
Though outwardly we are wasting away,
yet inwardly we are being renewed day by day.
For our light and momentary troubles
are achieving for us an eternal glory
that far outweighs them all.
So we fix our eyes not on what is seen,
but on what is unseen.
For what is seen is temporary,
but what is unseen is eternal.

2 Corinthians 4:16–18
(New International Version)

3

courage

Grace

Grant me that
graceful moment
in which pain
becomes learning
and tragedy, survivorship.

Let my tears
be as a river
or a mighty sea
floating my soul
beyond this rocky shore.

Kate Robinson

So You Mustn't Be Frightened

So you mustn't be frightened . . . if a sadness rises in front of you, larger than any you have ever seen; if an anxiety, like light and cloud-shadows, moves over your hands and over everything you do. You must realize that something is happening to you, that life has not forgotten you, that it holds you in its hand and will not let you fall. Why do you want to shut out of your life any uneasiness, any misery, any depression, since after all you don't know what work these conditions are doing inside you? Why do you want to persecute yourself with the question of where all this is coming from and where it is going? Since you know, after all, that you are in the midst of transitions and you wished for nothing so much as to change. If there is anything unhealthy in your reactions, just bear in mind that sickness is the means by which an organism frees itself from what is alien; so one must simply help it to be sick, to have its whole sickness and to break out with it, since that is the way it gets better. In you . . . so much is happening now; you must be patient like someone who is sick, and confident like someone who is recovering; for perhaps you are both. And more: you are also the doctor, who has to watch over himself. But in every sickness there are many days when the doctor can do nothing but wait. And that is what you, insofar as you are your own doctor, must now do, more than anything else.

Rainer Maria Rilke
(1875–1926)
translated by Stephen Mitchell

Facing the Facts

We are pulled, Gentle One, like a turkey wishbone in this balancing act of illness. We ping-pong between accepting and denying, giving up and fighting. Give us strength to find and face facts, for there is freedom and power in knowledge. Help us understand that *accepting* is not throwing in the towel; rather, through grace, *accepting* is like going to the bank to withdraw our savings . . . our spiritual, mental, and physical resources. As we make the transaction, we know You are our endless, bottomless, forever source.

Margaret Anne Huffman
(1941–2000)

Letting Go

Let go of the place that holds,
Let go of the place that flinches,
Let go of the place that controls,
Let go of the place that fears.
Just let the ground support me.
Listen, the wind is breathing in the trees.
Sensing the edge of soft and hard,
I follow the unseen path.
Walking in the dark night,
I practice faith,
building confidence in the unknown.
I practice courage,
accepting the vastness
of what I cannot see.

Stephanie Kaza

At Peace

Be tough in the way a blade of grass is:
rooted, willing to lean,
and at peace with what is around it.

Natalie Goldberg

Courage Is Not the Absence of Fear

I do not want [my children] to think, as I once did,
that courage is the absence of fear.
Courage is the strength to act wisely
when we are most afraid. . . .

Mary Fisher

Do the Best

When we do the best we can,
we never know what miracles await.

Helen Keller
(1880–1968)

Grief

When grief pours salt
into the wounds of life,
we must not hide from it.
We have to face its fury
head-on, wrestle with its
clawing anguish,
back and forth,
between depression
and desolation,
so that the pain doesn't
metastasize into anger,
overflowing our eyes,
flooding our hearts.
Experience and express
the sorrow.
Choose to accept its sting,
knowing that time
will anesthetize, scar tissue
form over incisions,
not as pliable, perhaps,
but just as strong as before.

Susan R. Norton

A Vailima Prayer

Give us grace and strength
to forbear and to persevere.
Give us courage and gaiety
and the quiet mind.
Spare to us our friends, soften
to us our enemies. Bless us
if it may be in all our
innocent endeavors. If it
may not, give us the strength
to encounter that which is to
come, that we may be brave
in peril, constant in tribulation,
temperate in wrath.
And in all changes of fortune
And down to the gates of death
Loyal and loving
To one another.

Robert Louis Stevenson
(1850–1894)

[AUTHOR'S NOTE: *Stevenson died in Vailima on the island of
Samoa, where he was known as Tusitala the Storyteller.*]

Stubborn Faith

There is every reason to give up and give in,
for this illness is rough.
When I falter, remind me that with You,
I am as resilient as violets
pushing up through pavement cracks.

Margaret Anne Huffman
(1941–2000)

Somehow

Life's struggle
can be puzzling now & then.

Somehow
at the most difficult times
we find wings to fly.

Corrine De Winter

When You Get into a Tight Place

When you get into a tight place
    and everything goes against you
    'til it seems as though
    you could not hang on a minute longer,
never give up then,
    for that is just the place and time
    that the tide will turn.

Harriet Beecher Stowe
(1811–1896)

Endurance

From moment to moment one can bear much.

Teresa of Ávila
(1515–1582)

Courage

You gain strength, courage, and confidence by every experience in which you really stop to look fear in the face. You are able to say to yourself, "I lived through this horror. I can take the next thing that comes along." You must do the thing you think you cannot do.

Eleanor Roosevelt
(1884–1962)

4

hope

Hope Will Come Again

Soft, like an April breeze,
hope will come to you
again. She will fill your
night with her autumn
moon; her soft, clear light
will bathe your sky
of all anxiety. Now she
lies beneath your
thoughts so near, yet so
far; but she will
come to you again! She will
fill your darkened
cloud with her crimson ray.
She will climb your
inner sky on silver wing:
and high above,
beyond all thoughts or dreams,
she will lift her
weary head and sing in ecstasy!

Thomas L. Reid

Hanging by a Thread

Recovery is slow, Gentle Healer, and we're discouraged, hopeless. Raise our eyes to spiderwebs spun in a corner and remind us that no hope is too small. It is of *kiven,* Hebrew for "hope: to twist or twine like a spiderweb." This is the quality of hope . . . amazing strength that looks at first like a fragile, insignificant strand. Yet think what it does for the spider. Help us twist our tiny-strand hope into sturdy ropes of commitment to taking the next, and the next step toward health.

Margaret Anne Huffman
(1941–2000)

New Horizon

Dream one more dream,
Hope one more hope,
Take one more step;
Do not falter or despair.

Sing one more song;
Dance one more dance.
Love once again,
Your God is always there.

Norma Woodbridge

Hope Is What Will Get You Through This

Hope is what will get you through this—
the hope that you can beat it.
If you lose your hope, the illness has won.
Don't give up without a fight.

Mary Katherine Devine

Hope

Bring me hope
in bright brass urns
of monsoon rain,
between the claps of thunder
under thoughts that fill the ponds
and swell the river
Bring me hope
and I will bloom
like a lotus in sun.

Lalita Noronha

The Essence of Touch

It's about the Spirit.
Where it goes.
Who it touches.
It holds us close and it sets us free.
We can choose to sit and wait
or we can stand and trust
that it will mend our broken wings and
welcome our lost souls.
This invisible force gives us hope,
offers us comfort, whispers our salvation.
It invites us among the angels and gives us
the confidence to fly.

Lori Eberhardy

Sowing, Reaping

We *must* believe small healing steps matter, Great En-
courager, for You say mountains can be budged with faith as
small as mustard seeds. Ah, though, there's nothing small about
a Scottish hillside blanketed with yellow mustard flowers. They
are tiny *and* mighty—a package deal with You at our elbow.
Forgive us when we don't recognize mustard-seed power in the
small accomplishments we are making as we move from illness
through recovery to restored health.

Too often, we confess, we wait for overnight drama and
overlook tiny flickers of change. They're begging to be noticed
and gathered into a radiant harvest of hope.

Margaret Anne Huffman
(1941–2000)

Spring Is My Faith

I ask in my fear
why this happened to me.
Yet I can't hold back
the praise that wells up inside.

I ask in my pain
why I must suffer.
Yet gratitude is the constant
motion within, and I know
the deep nourishment of spirit.

The cancer cells multiply
like flakes of snow.
My body is a waste of white.
Yet spring is my faith.
In the bright morning sun
the overnight snow glitters
and is gone.
The forsythia remains.

Ida Fasel

Faith

There is a sun that shines in my heart.
It is stronger than the coldest winter in my life.

Theresa Nault

Outside the Bone-Marrow Unit

It has been over a year since she waved
aside the wheelchair and walked in her own bright bones

out of that sterilized chamber: the butterfly
doors swung open and she stepped into air

that two weeks earlier could have killed her.
I'm worried that writing about cancer,

thinking about cancer, will start cancer
growing again inside her. Where in that sweet void,

where in those wide heavens
could it be hiding?

I stand on my toes and kiss one of my angels,
and in that kiss beg her

to take a stiff broom to this talk:
sweep the cancer back across the heavens;

please don't miss one crumb of it. Sweep
the cancer back into its black box of oblivion.

John Rybicki

An Assignment

One of the most effective ways to neutralize
medical pessimism is to find someone
who had the same problem you do
and is now healed.

Andrew Weil

Rejoice

And we rejoice in the hope of the glory of God.
Not only so, but we also rejoice in our sufferings,
because we know that suffering produces perseverance;
perseverance, character
and character, hope.

Romans 5:2–4
(New International Version)

For We Are Here,

not merely
to bloom in the light,
but rather, like trees,
to be weathered:
burned by heat, frozen by snow,
and though our hearts
have been broken,
still, we put out new leaves
in spring,
begin again.

Barbara Crooker

Hoping

Hoping is knowing that there is love,
it is trust in tomorrow
it is falling asleep
and waking again
when the sun rises.
In the midst of a gale at sea,
it is to discover land.
In the eyes of another
it is to see that he understands you . . .
As long as there still is hope
There will also be prayer . . .
And God will be holding you
in his hands.

Author unknown

5

healing

Rx

Right after the diagnosis, "You're sick," comes the blissful command, "Go to bed." No guilt. No argument. Just go to bed. Lie on white sheets. Sleep. Rouse and read a chapter of your book. Nap. Awaken to a cooler forehead and sip chamomile tea poured from the chubby brown pot. Doze. Say little. Listen to the rustle of your turning on the sheets, the rustle of pages as you read another chapter, the rustle of loved ones being quiet downstairs. The quiet is for you. Get well.

Martha K. Baker

In the House of the Sun

In the house of the sun there is
A yellow just for you; it shines
Even brighter when you are
Not looking or waiting.
In the house of the moon there is
A white just for you; it holds
Your worries, your fears, your wants;
It rocks them all to sleep.
In the house of your heart there are
So many colors we cannot count
Or name them; they swirl together
Endlessly healing, healing, healing.

Cassie Premo Steele

Get Well

Get well as rivers running,
spirits dancing under blue, blue skies.
Listen to the rain.
Begin again.
Go to where rose blossoms
drift into your heart and
nights are no longer too long.
Believe you can dance
in the darkness—
nothing will overshadow
your life.
God is with you in every moment in time.
Celebrate seaside moments
of peace
love
and joy
that echo your name
and hold your hand
the same way God does.
Get well.

Paula Timpson

Hippocratic Wisdom

Honor the healing power of nature.

Hippocrates
(ca. 460–377 BC)

Sanctuary

Close your eyes.
Grab hold of your imagination.
Tug on it 'til it cooperates, and
with its help, create a haven,
your own private sanctuary,
where you can escape to
for solace, courage
or strength of body and soul.

It could be a sheltered green garden,
a wooded glen or pebbled beach,
whatever scene nourishes you,
whatever sights and sounds calm you,
whatever regenerates you.

Know that in the blink of an eye,
the tick of a heart's clock,
you can go there.
Airline tickets aren't necessary.
Road maps can be stored away.
Advanced booking not required.

The only reservation you need make
is with yourself.

Susan R. Norton

For Healing

May we discover through pain and torment, the strength to
    live with grace and humor.
May we discover through doubt and anguish, the strength to
    live with dignity and holiness.
May we discover through suffering and fear, the strength to
    move toward healing.

May it come to pass that we be restored to health and to vigor.
May Life grant us wellness of body, spirit, and mind.
And if this cannot be so, may we find in this transformation
    and passage
moments of meaning, opportunities for love
and the deep and gracious calm that comes when we allow
    ourselves to move on.

Rabbi Rami Shapiro

This I Know

The wound: flesh or spirit deep
The choice: to quit or keep on
The way: accept and let go
The promise: to heal and grow.

Arlene Gay Levine

Why Not?

In the face of fear
let me hope

In the face of doubt
let me know

In the grip of loneliness
let me reach out

In the grip of pain
let me breathe

In spite of grief
let me smile

In spite of anger
let me pray.

Maryanne Hannan

Woman to Woman

I am no stranger.
I am a woman like you
mending after illness.
I would take the fear
palpable as a walnut
out of your body,
the fear that something
can erase our breath.
Somewhere inside
a wisdom larger than us
knows the course of our lives
and carries the weight
of our pain and fear,
and offers with tender hands
the faith and understanding
that leads to healing.

Marian Olson

For a Dear One at a Dark Time

Your world seems empty now: a puzzle with pieces
you thought made you complete, now missing.
If I could make you listen, in your loneliest hour,
the doves continue to coo and soft breezes
still strum their spring song on budding branches.
If I could help you see, in your lightless prison,
the perfection of a powder-blue–sky day
has not gone away and the courageous yellow face
of a solitary dandelion defies the gardener's rake.

If I could urge you to inhale, despite your clenched chest,
you'd be healed by the green tonic of mown grass
or even the humble aroma of a potato
baking in the oven just for you.
If I could I would teach you to taste the salt of your tears
and explore their source, to feel the jagged edges
of your newly broken heart, and with those same hands,
use the thread of your pain to sew a stronger version
whole again.

Arlene Gay Levine

The Best Cure

The best cure
for the body
is to quiet the mind.

Napoleon Bonaparte
(1769–1821)

Twilight Cure

Hush, this is the soft hour
Let us settle down
Hush, this is the cadence of peace
Let us breathe deeply
Hush, this is the healing time
Let us go within
Hush, this is the prayer
Let us convalesce.

Arlene Gay Levine

Live Quietly

God help us to live quietly
  Amidst the clamor,
    To find that slower pace
      that gentler place
     Where our hearts can listen,
     Where we can listen to
     Our hearts.
      Amen.

Jim Croegaert

Be Patient

Of course you are anxious to feel better, but don't be impatient. Healing takes time. Despite great advances in medicine, the biggest part of your recovery is attributable to the enormous healing power inside you. The body heals itself according to its own timetable—anxious thoughts never hasten recuperation.

Criswell Freeman

Renaissance

Coming back to life
like the earth in spring,
energy flows
in a gentle resurgence
throughout my being.

Coming back to life,
my long-smoldering soul
is all aflame, rekindled
by a tender touch
and time.

Abigail Brandt

For a Friend Lying in Intensive Care Waiting for Her White Blood Cells to Rejuvenate After a Bone-Marrow Transplant

The jonquils. They come back. They split the earth with
    their green swords, bearing cups of light.
The forsythia comes back, spraying its thin whips with
    blossom, one loud yellow shout.
The robins. They come back. They pull the sun on the
    silver thread of their song.
The iris come back. They dance in the soft air in silken
    gowns of midnight blue.
The lilacs come back. They trail their perfume like a scarf
    of violet chiffon.
And the leaves come back, on every tree and bush, millions
    and millions of small green hands applauding your return.

Barbara Crooker

Angel Wings

Wrap yourself in angel wings,
Settling deep within strength and solace.
Wrap yourself in angel wings,
Composed in a graceful tune to life.
Be comforted,
Be guarded,
Be well.

Annie Dougherty

Sink into Stillness

As you close your eyes,
sink into stillness.
Let these periods of rest and respite
reassure your mind
that all its frantic fantasies
were but the dreams
of fever that has passed away.
Let it be still
and thankfully accept its healing.
No more fearful dreams will come,
now that you rest in God.

A Course in Miracles
(Workbook, p. 197)

Surrender to Wonder

In Wonder was I conceived
and in Wonder have I found my being.
Thus I call upon you, the Source of Wonder
to open my heart to healing.

In you I discover the mystery of Life
and the necessity of Death.
In you I see all things and their opposites
not as warring parties
but as partners in a dance
whose rhythm is none other
than the beating of my own soul.

Denial may come, but so too will acceptance.
Anger may come, but so too will calm.
I have bargained with my fears
and found them unwilling to compromise.
So now I turn to you,
to the Wonder that is my True Nature.

My tears will pass
and so will my laughter.
But I will not be silenced,

for I will sing praises of Wonder
through sickness and health;
knowing that in the end,
this too shall pass.

Rabbi Rami Shapiro

6

reflections

I Live in Wonder

I live in wonder
of my own frailty and
the simple ways it teaches me
to be still.

I breathe the gentle whisper
of patience learned at rest
on the sea, becalmed.

Land and feet will meet again,
no hurry. I float in
the shimmering
stillness, marveling
at how fragile, and yet
how seaworthy,
I have become.

Pamela Burke

In the Midst of Greatest Sorrow

It is a mark of faith, nobility, and courage to turn a minus into a plus and to discover positive good in the midst of greatest sorrow.

Dale E. Turner

Tomorrow

It has often been said that in our lives
There are seasons for all things.
To laugh, to love, to share our joy
And the happiness life brings.

But there are times when darkness comes
And shadows the fragile heart.
We courageously fight and silently pray
For our healing time to start.

It is at these moments when our lives are filled
With pain or strife or sorrow
That God's gracious understanding is revealed
In a gift we call "tomorrow."

A new day brimming with possibilities
And hope sent from above,
Bestowed to help ease the cross we bear
With Heaven's unbending love.

Heather Berry

In the Midst of Pain

My chemotherapy is at a difficult point.
I am tired of being tired and sick.
Since I have so little energy, I try to focus on small pleasures
so that I feel like I still have a life and the disease is not taking
    over.

When I don't accomplish as much as I want, I find myself angry
    at life
and jealous of those who can do what I do not have the
    energy for,
trying hard not to let this hideous disease control me.
I fight melancholy on a daily basis.
It's a struggle to live on the bright side of life
when I don't have the energy to lift a dust rag.

The will to heal comes from within.
To question illness leads to confusion and despair.
To accept the gamble of life brings understanding
and appreciation of what it is to live.
I resent pity because so many suffer more than I do.

I have truly lived my life fully.
Most people live without disease and its consequences

but many of them don't live as full a life as those who are ill. We, who struggle daily, appreciate all that we have.

Virginia Lynn Eathorne

Pain

When we must live with pain
that dark-robed visitor
becomes more bearable
as it grows more familiar.
We begin to sense how long
we must endure its presence,
we understand when to struggle
against its grim power
and when to submit.
Through pain we learn about
our bodies and our spirits.
Pain cleanses us, the edge
of its robe sweeping away
regret, confusion, and pettiness.
And when pain parts from us,
releasing us from its grip,
we are left empty, purified,
and grateful for small pleasures.

SuzAnne C. Cole

The Best We Can Do

A rosebush wilting in July heat
does not blame the earth, lets its roots
search deep for the waters of life.
After its surge of golden glory
the bare oak does not accuse
the winter's frigid air, invites
the wind to sing hymns through
its naked boughs.

The best we can do is to allow,
learn to love the changing
landscape of our lives.
Episodes of dark and doubt
are unexpected guests, asking only
to be welcomed for a while,
these gods in disguise
who guide us home.

Arlene Gay Levine

Permanent Gifts

Sometimes
        the presence of God
                sweeps through us
    like a gust of autumn wind
                        stripping away
                            what we thought was essential.

The golden leaves of our lives
            lie scattered at our feet
                and we are left
                    looking at the bare trunk
                            of our existence.

In this stripping
    we touch the core of who we are
            and know we will survive the winter.

It is only through this loss
        that we discover
                    what we can never lose.

Molly Srode

Hope from a Cancer Survivor

I gave up innocence
for all of this—
a life without guarantees,
but in exchange
I planted the seeds
of eternity,
in trust and belief,
in homage to grief,
in the endless renewability
of surrender.

Susan Moon

What Does Not Destroy Me

What does not destroy me
makes me stronger.

Friedrich Nietzsche
(1844–1900)

A Meditation on Acceptance

Whatever is in harmony with you, O Universe,
is in harmony with me.
Whatever comes in due season for you
is not too early or too late for me.
What your seasons bring is fruit for me,
for all things come from you and return to you.

Marcus Aurelius
Meditations, Book IV, 23, translated by Maryanne Hannan

What Really Counts

We cannot tell what may happen
to us in the strange medley of life.
But we can decide what happens in us,
how we take it, what we do with it—
and that is what really counts in the end.

Joseph Fort Newton

Think Positive

The longer we dwell on our misfortunes,
the greater is their power to harm us.

Voltaire
(1694–1778)

Worrying

I think these difficult times have helped me to understand better than before how infinitely rich and beautiful life is in every way, and that so many things that one goes around worrying about are of no importance whatsoever.

Isak Dinesen
(1885–1962)

Difficulties

Difficulties are God's errands and trainers, and only through them can one come to the fullness of humanity.

Henry Ward Beecher
(1813–1887)

The Sources of Human Strength

Suffering and sorrow remain the supreme mystery of life. A great source of steadiness can be found in the knowledge that countless others have faced precisely the same problems without being utterly defeated in spirit. No wound of the body or soul is unique or entirely new, and others with similar scars have something to say to us. Among the sources of human strength is a resource unequaled—the friendship of any person who has preceded another through a similar valley who can quietly say, "I understand."

Dale E. Turner

In Sickness

It is in sickness
(not in health)
that our true nature
shows its face,
shines a light
upon our shadowy
still-beating hearts.

You have risen
up out of darkness
to see this truth.
You are a brave dancer
moving your body
to the music
God continues to make.

Peter Markus

Steadfast Hope

Out of times
of tremendous trial
sprout seasons
of abundant
growth.

Joan Marie Arbogast

When One Door Closes

When one door closes another door
opens; but we often look so longingly
and so regretfully upon the door that
closed, that we fail to see the one that
has opened for us.

Helen Keller
(1880–1968)

The Way of All Flesh

The beginning is new
fresh with promise

The middle is ours
to wrest meaning from pain
comfort from confusion

The end is forgiveness
In the end is Love

Maryanne Hannan

Your Daily Task

Have courage for the
great sorrows of life and
patience for the small
ones; and when you have
laboriously accomplished
your daily task, go to
sleep in peace.
God is awake.

Victor Hugo
(1802–1885)

Attitude

The greatest discovery of my generation
is that a human being can alter his life
by altering the attitude of his mind.

William James
(1842–1910)

Reflect

Reflect on the dark
where fear is lost.

Reflect on the dark
where light begins.

Reflect on the dark
where gold is dancing.

Janine Canan

7
gratitude

The Guest House

This being human is a guest house.
Every morning a new arrival.

A joy, a depression, a meanness,
some momentary awareness comes
as an unexpected visitor.

Welcome and entertain them all!
Even if they're a crowd of sorrows,
who violently sweep your house
empty of its furniture,
still, treat each guest honorably.
He may be clearing you out
for some new delight.

The dark thought, the shame, the malice,
meet them at the door laughing,
and invite them in.

Be grateful for whoever comes,
because each has been sent
as a guide from beyond.

Rumi
(1207–1273)
translated by Coleman Barks

Peace Begins Within

Sometimes it's the little things that mean the most: the song of a bird, a warm breeze blowing through the trees, a friendly voice on the other end of a telephone, a note written by a friend to us when we need encouragement, the wag of a dog's tail as we come home from a hard day at work. These things are intangible—we cannot put a price tag on what they mean to us or how they help us to feel abiding peace even in the midst of turmoil. When I am tempted to lose control and get angry or bitter, I must remember the things that make me happy, and become peaceful within. No matter what the outward appearances, I can always return to these things, and feel the joy that comes from them.

Today, I am thankful for the little things that bring peace from within.

Heather Parkins

To the Gardener of the World

Thank you for arousing in us
a hunger to live,
for bringing us to rest
in the shade of your Tree of Life,
for awakening in us
the light of your promise,
for breathing into our weary limbs
your spirit of refreshment and renewal.

Father John B. Giuliani

Unknown Blessings

Give thanks
for unknown
blessings already
on their way.

Native American saying

The Gifts of Illness

In illness I must slow down,
rest, treat myself with tenderness—
hard things to do sometimes
without the excuse, "I'm sick."
In illness I must rely on others;
exposing my vulnerability,
trusting others with my needs,
is good medicine for my soul.

Even in physical illness,
I can be spiritually healthy,
curious about the world,
and grateful for small gifts—
fresh crisp bed linens,
plump feather pillows,
hand-squeezed orange juice,
chamomile tea and toast,
a book of prayers,
a call from a friend,
a rental movie I missed.

I didn't choose to be ill—but
I can choose to accept its gifts.

SuzAnne C. Cole

A Good Prognosis

It helps that I have a good prognosis; I focus on that and on listening to what I might learn from this experience. I am beginning to more fully appreciate each day as it unfolds, something that I have always strived for but could always put off in the innocence of time stretched forever ahead of me. That innocence was shattered, and I have to deal with that loss, but the gain from living more fully in the moment provides meaning. Thank you.

Sally Rosloff

Sufi Saying

When the heart weeps for what it has lost,
The Spirit laughs for what it has found.

Author unknown

Rainbows

A true sign of the miracles in God's world occurs when a rainbow appears, bright and shining, through the darkest of cloudy days. We have sought pots of gold at the end of them, and have watched them appear in waterfalls, crystals, and other places. We never know when a rainbow will appear, and like the wonders of a rainbow full of its spectrum of color, we must remember that the one who made the rainbows beautiful also made us. We can be like a rainbow: full of color, shining through adversity.

Today I give thanks for the unique colors in my world, and give thanks that I am able to enjoy them.

Heather Parkins

Cancer Caregiver

Husband
To have and to hold
In sickness and in health
We had ten good years of health
Now is the time of sickness
You hold my hand
Do things for me you never imagined
Your love shines through every hour of every day
Lover, Husband, Caregiver
Have I told you today that I love you?

Mary Platt

Divine Gifts

Life is so generous a giver, but we, judging its gifts by their
    covering,
cast them away as ugly or heavy, or hard. Remove the
    covering,
and you will find beneath it a living splendor, woven of love,
by wisdom, with power.

Welcome it, grasp it, and you touch the angel's hand that brings
    it to you.
Everything we call a trial, a sorrow, or a duty, believe me,
that angel's hand is there; the gift is there, and the wonder of
    an overshadowing presence. Our joys too: be not content
    with them as joys.
They too conceal diviner gifts.

Fra Giovanni Giocondo

So Very Blessed

Cancer is such a weird thing . . .
it has taught me each day is a gift
that cannot be taken for granted.
We feel so lucky, so fortunate, and so very blessed.
We live each day and love each moment.

Joanie Guggenmos

Your Monumental Kindness

I was wounded,
and you took me
into your heart.

I was lost,
and you led
me along.

I was broken,
and you
reached out
a hand.

Susan Landon

Handicaps

I thank God for my handicaps,
for, through them,
I have found myself,
my work, and my God.

Helen Keller
(1880–1968)

8

inspiration

May You Be Well

May the morning sun shine in your heart.
May the blue-white sky
be in
all your days.
May the moon and the stars
shine on all your nights.
Delight yourself.
God's gifts
are yours
every day.
May quiet smiles brighten you.
May you be well.

Paula Timpson

Earth, Teach Me

Earth, teach me stillness
    as the grasses are stilled with light.
Earth, teach me suffering
    as old stones suffer with memory.
Earth, teach me humility
    as blossoms are humble with beginning.
Earth, teach me caring
    as the mother who secures her young.
Earth, teach me courage
    as the tree that stands all alone.
Earth, teach me limitation
    as the ant that crawls on the ground.
Earth, teach me freedom
    as the eagle that soars in the sky.
Earth, teach me resignation
    as the leaves that die in the fall.
Earth, teach me regeneration
    as the seed that rises in the spring.
Earth, teach me to forget myself
    as melted snow forgets its life.

Earth, teach me to remember kindness
as dry fields weep with rain.

Ute prayer

Stay Well

Let your soul create
a sanctuary where
all dreams are possible
and life is grand as God's glory.
The beach stretches
before you.
You are strong as the sea's song.
Whitecaps travel and return.
May you never
feel alone or
lose sight of the
sacred seasons of your soul.
Stay well.

Paula Timpson

One Year to Live

If I had but one year to live;
One year to help; one year to give;
One year to love; one year to bless;
One year of better things to stress;
One year to sing; one year to smile;
To brighten earth a little while;
I think that I would spend each day,
In just the very selfsame way
That I do now. For from afar
The call may come to cross the bar
At any time, and I must be
Prepared to meet eternity.
So if I have a year to live,
Or just a day in which to give
A pleasant smile, a helping hand,
A mind that tries to understand
A fellow-creature when in need,
'Tis one with me,—I take no heed;
But try to live each day He sends
To serve my gracious Master's ends.

Mary Davis Reed

Breast-Cancer Benefit

What matters is not the cancer.
Nor is it the bald head,
the misshapen blouse,
the scarred chest,
the ashen skin
that does not seem to fit
the sunken cheeks.

It is how these women laugh and nod
and agree about cancer
as if it is the daily news, a new joke,
an old truth;
how they tilt their heads in a way
that says grace,
how they walk with an air that says
I am miraculous,
how their partners look as if
they might just be overcome with agony
and joy
if given just one more moment to watch
as these women bask in life.

Rosie Molinary

Resting Place

Today is a resting place on my journey, Lord.
Today I'm relaxing my hold on worry,
loosening the ties that bind me to this illness
letting go of all my complaints and apprehension.
They can simmer on the back burner—provide tomorrow's
   stew.

Today I'm remembering
old friends—laughs and tears we shared;
old beaus—dancing in moonlight;
old days when my body and I had some wonderful times
enjoying sunshine, cool water, the treasures of the snow.

Hold my hand today, Lord, as I give thanks
for roses and babies and long swirly skirts;
for twinkling eyes and strong arms and soft voices—
for memories.

Hold my hand tomorrow, too, Lord.
Float me in the safe waters of Your love.

   Joan Eheart Cinelli

Before It Is Too Late

If you have a tender message,
    Or a loving word to say,
Do not wait till you forget it,
    But whisper it today;
The tender word unspoken,
    The letter never sent,
The long-forgotten messages,
    The wealth of love unspent—
For these some hearts are breaking,
    For these some loved ones wait;
So show them that you care for them
    Before it is too late.

Frank Herbert Sweet

What Cancer Cannot Do

Cancer is limited . . .

It cannot cripple love,
It cannot shatter hope,
It cannot erode faith,
It cannot destroy peace,
It cannot kill friendship,
It cannot suppress memories,
It cannot silence courage,
It cannot invade the soul,
It cannot steal eternal life,
It cannot conquer the spirit!

Author unknown

Rejoice

This is the day which the Lord hath made;
we will rejoice and be glad in it.

Psalms 118:24
(King James Version)

A New Dimension

When we face a personal calamity and handle it well, we add a new dimension to our character. The pain and trouble we shrink from—and try to escape—when used wisely, often turns out to be the source of the best in our life and also adds to the joy of living.

Dale E. Turner

Perspective

Rather than focusing
on what has been lost,
Dear God, help me to be grateful
for how much I still have.

June Cotner Graves

Restoration Zone

In the aftermath of a major illness, it takes energy and courage to rebuild, Great Architect of our lives. How amazing that Your gift of courage translates *wishing* into *hoping,* the active word we need; it turns worry into energy and fear into determination.

Assure us that it's okay to be afraid, for fear is honest; so are anger, disappointment, grief. Help us recognize feelings as potential fuel that can be turned into reconstruction tools. Through Your grace, we've courageously faced *what is* and are now off to see *what can be.*

Margaret Anne Huffman
(1941–2000)

The Road

Here is the road: the light
comes and goes then returns again.
Be gentle with your fellow travelers
as they move through the world of stone and stars
whirling with you yet every one alone.
The road waits.
Do not ask questions but when it invites you
to dance at daybreak, say yes.
Each step is the journey; a single note the song.

Arlene Gay Levine

For As Long As It Matters

Here's the thing.
In every life crisis, there's that moment
when you must choose whether
to trade down to despair, or up to joy.
I will choose joy.
From now on,
with whatever I've got left,
I'll look for occasions of laughter.
I'll blow soap bubbles
and run barefoot on the beach.
I'll make a list of things to laugh at.
Maybe I'll even dye my hair red.
When I talk, I'll smile.
I'll see that there is always laughter in my voice.
Every day.
As long as I have.
As long as it matters,
I'll choose joy.

Dorothy Wilhelm

Author Index

Permissions and Acknowledgments

Grateful acknowledgment is made to the authors and publishers for the use of the following material. Every effort has been made to contact original sources. If notified, the publishers will be pleased to rectify an omission in future editions.

Joan Marie Arbogast for "Steadfast Hope."

Martha K. Baker for "Rx."

Bantam Doubleday Dell Publishing Group, Inc., for "Before It Is Too Late" by Frank Herbert Sweet, and "One Year to Live" by Mary Davis Reed, from *Poems That Touch the Heart,* compiled by A. L. Alexander. Copyright © 1941 by Bantam Doubleday Dell.

Coleman Barks for "The Guest House" by Jalal Al-Din Rumi from *The Essential Rumi,* translated by Coleman Barks, published by HarperSanFrancisco. Copyright © 1995 by Coleman Barks. Reprinted by kind permission of Coleman Barks.

Heather Berry for "Tomorrow."

Abigail Brandt for "Renaissance."

Pamela Burke for "I Live in Wonder."

Janine Canan for "Reflect," excerpted from *In the Palace of Creation: Selected Works 1969–1999,* by Janine Canan, published by Scars Publications. Copyright © 2003 by Janine Canan. Reprinted by kind permission of Janine Canan.

Joan Eheart Cinelli for "Resting Place."

SuzAnne C. Cole for "The Gifts of Illness" and "Pain."

Deborah Gordon Cooper for "Prayer in Time of Trouble."

Jim Croegaert for "Live Quietly."

Barbara Crooker for "For a Friend Lying in Intensive Care Waiting for Her White Blood Cells to Rejuvenate After a Bone-Marrow Transplant," and "For We Are Here."

Phyllis Joy Davison for "A Life Jacket."

Corrine De Winter for "Somehow."

Mary Katherine Devine for "Hope Is What Will Get You Through This."

Annie Dougherty for "Angel Wings."

Virginia Lynn Eathorne for "In the Midst of Pain."

Lori Eberhardy for "Angel Embrace," "The Essence of Touch," "Great Expectations," "A Quiet Comfort," and "Safe Passage."

Ida Fasel for "Spring Is My Faith."

Father John B. Giuliani for "To the Gardener of the World."

June Cotner Graves for "Perspective."

Joanie Guggenmos for "So Very Blessed."

Maryanne Hannan for "A Meditation on Acceptance" (translation of Marcus Aurelius), "The Way of All Flesh," and "Why Not?"

The Reverend Gary W. Huffman for "Facing the Facts," "Hanging by a Thread," "Hearing with Hearts of Faith," "Restoration Zone," "Sowing, Reaping," "Stubborn Faith," "Take My Hand," and "Testing, Testing . . ." by Margaret Anne Huffman.

Stephanie Kaza for "Letting Go," excerpted from *The Attentive Heart: Conversation with Trees* by Stephanie Kaza. Copyright © 1993 by Stephanie Kaza, published by Ballantine Books. Used by kind permission of Stephanie Kaza.

Susan Landon for "Your Monumental Kindness."

Arlene Gay Levine for "For a Dear One at a Dark Time," "The Best We Can Do," "The Road," "This I Know," and "Twilight Cure."

Jill Noblit MacGregor for "From Your Friend."

Peter Markus for "In Sickness."

Sylvia LeFort Masi for "3 AM."

Rosie Molinary for "Breast-Cancer Benefit."

Susan Moon for "Hope from a Cancer Survivor."

Theresa Nault for "Faith."

Lalita Noronha for "Hope."

Susan R. Norton for "Grief" and "Sanctuary."

Marian Olson for "Woman to Woman."

Heather Parkins for "Peace Begins Within" and "Rainbows."

Eugene Platt for "Cancer Caregiver" by Mary Platt.

Patricia M. Poland for "Still Waters."

Thomas L. Reid for "Hope Will Come Again."

Kate Robinson for "Grace."

Sally Rosloff for "A Good Prognosis."

Gwen Tremain Runyard for "To a Good Friend."

John Rybicki for "Outside the Bone-Marrow Unit."

Sara Sanderson for "Angel Promise."

Marion Schoeberlein for "Each Day You Call My Heart, O God."

Rabbi Rami Shapiro for "For Healing," "Surrender to Wonder," and "Unending Love."

Joan Shroyer-Keno for "Steps."

Molly Srode for "Permanent Gifts."

Cassie Premo Steele for "In the House of the Sun."

Paula Timpson for "Get Well," "May You Be Well," and "Stay Well."

Dale E. Turner for "In the Midst of Greatest Sorrow" and "The Sources of Human Strength," excerpted from *Another Way* by Dale E. Turner, published by High Tide Press. Copyright © 2001 by Dale E. Turner; and "A New Dimension" by Dale E. Turner, from *Wisdom Through the Ages* by Helen Granat, published by Miklen Press. Copyright © 1998 by Helen Granat. Reprinted by kind permission of Dale E. Turner.

Dorothy Wilhelm for "For As Long As It Matters."

Norma Woodbridge for "New Horizon."